CLUE SCO

SUSPECTS					
Col. Mustard					
Prof. Plum					
Mr. Green					
Mrs. Peacock					
Miss Scarlett					
Mrs. White					
WEAPONS					
Knife					
Candlestick					
Revolver					
Rope					
Lead Pipe					
Wrench					
ROOMS					
Hall					
Lounge					
Dining Room					
Kitchen					
Ball Room					
Conservatory					
Billard Room					
Library					
Study					

CLUE SCORE SHEET

SUSPECTS						
Col. Mustard						
Prof. Plum						
Mr. Green						
Mrs. Peacock						
Miss Scarlett						
Mrs. White						
WEAPONS						
Knife						
Candlestick						
Revolver						
Rope						
Lead Pipe						
Wrench						
ROOMS						
Hall						
Lounge						
Dining Room						
Kitchen						
Ball Room						
Conservatory						
Billard Room						
Library						
Study						

CLUE SCORE SHEET

SUSPECTS					
Col. Mustard					
Prof. Plum					
Mr. Green					
Mrs. Peacock					
Miss Scarlett					
Mrs. White					
WEAPONS					
Knife					
Candlestick					
Revolver					
Rope					
Lead Pipe					
Wrench					
ROOMS					
Hall					
Lounge					
Dining Room					
Kitchen					
Ball Room					
Conservatory					
Billard Room					
Library					
Study					

CLUE SCORE SHEET

SUSPECTS						
Col. Mustard						
Prof. Plum						
Mr. Green						
Mrs. Peacock						
Miss Scarlett						
Mrs. White						
WEAPONS						
Knife						
Candlestick						
Revolver						
Rope						
Lead Pipe						
Wrench						
ROOMS						
Hall						
Lounge						
Dining Room						
Kitchen						
Ball Room						
Conservatory						
Billard Room						
Library						
Study						

CLUE SCORE SHEET

SUSPECTS					
Col. Mustard					
Prof. Plum					
Mr. Green					
Mrs. Peacock					
Miss Scarlett					
Mrs. White					
WEAPONS					
Knife					
Candlestick					
Revolver					
Rope					
Lead Pipe					
Wrench					
ROOMS					
Hall					
Lounge					
Dining Room					
Kitchen					
Ball Room					
Conservatory					
Billard Room					
Library					
Study					

CLUE SCORE SHEET

SUSPECTS					
Col. Mustard					
Prof. Plum					
Mr. Green					
Mrs. Peacock					
Miss Scarlett					
Mrs. White					
WEAPONS					
Knife					
Candlestick					
Revolver					
Rope					
Lead Pipe					
Wrench					
ROOMS					
Hall					
Lounge					
Dining Room					
Kitchen					
Ball Room					
Conservatory					
Billard Room					
Library					
Study					

CLUE SCORE SHEET

SUSPECTS						
Col. Mustard						
Prof. Plum						
Mr. Green						
Mrs. Peacock						
Miss Scarlett						
Mrs. White						
WEAPONS						
Knife						
Candlestick						
Revolver						
Rope						
Lead Pipe						
Wrench						
ROOMS						
Hall						
Lounge						
Dining Room						
Kitchen						
Ball Room						
Conservatory						
Billard Room						
Library						
Study						

CLUE SCORE SHEET

SUSPECTS						
Col. Mustard						
Prof. Plum						
Mr. Green						
Mrs. Peacock						
Miss Scarlett						
Mrs. White						
WEAPONS						
Knife						
Candlestick						
Revolver						
Rope						
Lead Pipe						
Wrench						
ROOMS						
Hall						
Lounge						
Dining Room						
Kitchen						
Ball Room						
Conservatory						
Billard Room						
Library						
Study						

CLUE SCORE SHEET

SUSPECTS						
Col. Mustard						
Prof. Plum						
Mr. Green						
Mrs. Peacock						
Miss Scarlett						
Mrs. White						
WEAPONS						
Knife						
Candlestick						
Revolver						
Rope						
Lead Pipe						
Wrench						
ROOMS						
Hall						
Lounge						
Dining Room						
Kitchen						
Ball Room						
Conservatory						
Billard Room						
Library						
Study						

CLUE SCORE SHEET

SUSPECTS					
Col. Mustard					
Prof. Plum					
Mr. Green					
Mrs. Peacock					
Miss Scarlett					
Mrs. White					

WEAPONS					
Knife					
Candlestick					
Revolver					
Rope					
Lead Pipe					
Wrench					

ROOMS					
Hall					
Lounge					
Dining Room					
Kitchen					
Ball Room					
Conservatory					
Billard Room					
Library					
Study					

CLUE SCORE SHEET

SUSPECTS					
Col. Mustard					
Prof. Plum					
Mr. Green					
Mrs. Peacock					
Miss Scarlett					
Mrs. White					
WEAPONS					
Knife					
Candlestick					
Revolver					
Rope					
Lead Pipe					
Wrench					
ROOMS					
Hall					
Lounge					
Dining Room					
Kitchen					
Ball Room					
Conservatory					
Billard Room					
Library					
Study					

CLUE SCORE SHEET

SUSPECTS					
Col. Mustard					
Prof. Plum					
Mr. Green					
Mrs. Peacock					
Miss Scarlett					
Mrs. White					
WEAPONS					
Knife					
Candlestick					
Revolver					
Rope					
Lead Pipe					
Wrench					
ROOMS					
Hall					
Lounge					
Dining Room					
Kitchen					
Ball Room					
Conservatory					
Billard Room					
Library					
Study					

CLUE SCORE SHEET

SUSPECTS					
Col. Mustard					
Prof. Plum					
Mr. Green					
Mrs. Peacock					
Miss Scarlett					
Mrs. White					
WEAPONS					
Knife					
Candlestick					
Revolver					
Rope					
Lead Pipe					
Wrench					
ROOMS					
Hall					
Lounge					
Dining Room					
Kitchen					
Ball Room					
Conservatory					
Billard Room					
Library					
Study					

CLUE SCORE SHEET

SUSPECTS					
Col. Mustard					
Prof. Plum					
Mr. Green					
Mrs. Peacock					
Miss Scarlett					
Mrs. White					
WEAPONS					
Knife					
Candlestick					
Revolver					
Rope					
Lead Pipe					
Wrench					
ROOMS					
Hall					
Lounge					
Dining Room					
Kitchen					
Ball Room					
Conservatory					
Billard Room					
Library					
Study					

CLUE SCORE SHEET

SUSPECTS					
Col. Mustard					
Prof. Plum					
Mr. Green					
Mrs. Peacock					
Miss Scarlett					
Mrs. White					
WEAPONS					
Knife					
Candlestick					
Revolver					
Rope					
Lead Pipe					
Wrench					
ROOMS					
Hall					
Lounge					
Dining Room					
Kitchen					
Ball Room					
Conservatory					
Billard Room					
Library					
Study					

CLUE SCORE SHEET

SUSPECTS						
Col. Mustard						
Prof. Plum						
Mr. Green						
Mrs. Peacock						
Miss Scarlett						
Mrs. White						
WEAPONS						
Knife						
Candlestick						
Revolver						
Rope						
Lead Pipe						
Wrench						
ROOMS						
Hall						
Lounge						
Dining Room						
Kitchen						
Ball Room						
Conservatory						
Billard Room						
Library						
Study						

CLUE SCORE SHEET

SUSPECTS					
Col. Mustard					
Prof. Plum					
Mr. Green					
Mrs. Peacock					
Miss Scarlett					
Mrs. White					
WEAPONS					
Knife					
Candlestick					
Revolver					
Rope					
Lead Pipe					
Wrench					
ROOMS					
Hall					
Lounge					
Dining Room					
Kitchen					
Ball Room					
Conservatory					
Billard Room					
Library					
Study					

CLUE SCORE SHEET

SUSPECTS						
Col. Mustard						
Prof. Plum						
Mr. Green						
Mrs. Peacock						
Miss Scarlett						
Mrs. White						
WEAPONS						
Knife						
Candlestick						
Revolver						
Rope						
Lead Pipe						
Wrench						
ROOMS						
Hall						
Lounge						
Dining Room						
Kitchen						
Ball Room						
Conservatory						
Billard Room						
Library						
Study						

CLUE SCORE SHEET

SUSPECTS					
Col. Mustard					
Prof. Plum					
Mr. Green					
Mrs. Peacock					
Miss Scarlett					
Mrs. White					
WEAPONS					
Knife					
Candlestick					
Revolver					
Rope					
Lead Pipe					
Wrench					
ROOMS					
Hall					
Lounge					
Dining Room					
Kitchen					
Ball Room					
Conservatory					
Billard Room					
Library					
Study					

CLUE SCORE SHEET

SUSPECTS					
Col. Mustard					
Prof. Plum					
Mr. Green					
Mrs. Peacock					
Miss Scarlett					
Mrs. White					
WEAPONS					
Knife					
Candlestick					
Revolver					
Rope					
Lead Pipe					
Wrench					
ROOMS					
Hall					
Lounge					
Dining Room					
Kitchen					
Ball Room					
Conservatory					
Billard Room					
Library					
Study					

CLUE SCORE SHEET

SUSPECTS						
Col. Mustard						
Prof. Plum						
Mr. Green						
Mrs. Peacock						
Miss Scarlett						
Mrs. White						
WEAPONS						
Knife						
Candlestick						
Revolver						
Rope						
Lead Pipe						
Wrench						
ROOMS						
Hall						
Lounge						
Dining Room						
Kitchen						
Ball Room						
Conservatory						
Billard Room						
Library						
Study						

CLUE SCORE SHEET

SUSPECTS					
Col. Mustard					
Prof. Plum					
Mr. Green					
Mrs. Peacock					
Miss Scarlett					
Mrs. White					
WEAPONS					
Knife					
Candlestick					
Revolver					
Rope					
Lead Pipe					
Wrench					
ROOMS					
Hall					
Lounge					
Dining Room					
Kitchen					
Ball Room					
Conservatory					
Billard Room					
Library					
Study					

CLUE SCORE SHEET

SUSPECTS						
Col. Mustard						
Prof. Plum						
Mr. Green						
Mrs. Peacock						
Miss Scarlett						
Mrs. White						
WEAPONS						
Knife						
Candlestick						
Revolver						
Rope						
Lead Pipe						
Wrench						
ROOMS						
Hall						
Lounge						
Dining Room						
Kitchen						
Ball Room						
Conservatory						
Billard Room						
Library						
Study						

CLUE SCORE SHEET

SUSPECTS						
Col. Mustard						
Prof. Plum						
Mr. Green						
Mrs. Peacock						
Miss Scarlett						
Mrs. White						
WEAPONS						
Knife						
Candlestick						
Revolver						
Rope						
Lead Pipe						
Wrench						
ROOMS						
Hall						
Lounge						
Dining Room						
Kitchen						
Ball Room						
Conservatory						
Billard Room						
Library						
Study						

CLUE SCORE SHEET

SUSPECTS					
Col. Mustard					
Prof. Plum					
Mr. Green					
Mrs. Peacock					
Miss Scarlett					
Mrs. White					
WEAPONS					
Knife					
Candlestick					
Revolver					
Rope					
Lead Pipe					
Wrench					
ROOMS					
Hall					
Lounge					
Dining Room					
Kitchen					
Ball Room					
Conservatory					
Billard Room					
Library					
Study					

CLUE SCORE SHEET

SUSPECTS						
Col. Mustard						
Prof. Plum						
Mr. Green						
Mrs. Peacock						
Miss Scarlett						
Mrs. White						
WEAPONS						
Knife						
Candlestick						
Revolver						
Rope						
Lead Pipe						
Wrench						
ROOMS						
Hall						
Lounge						
Dining Room						
Kitchen						
Ball Room						
Conservatory						
Billard Room						
Library						
Study						

CLUE SCORE SHEET

SUSPECTS						
Col. Mustard						
Prof. Plum						
Mr. Green						
Mrs. Peacock						
Miss Scarlett						
Mrs. White						
WEAPONS						
Knife						
Candlestick						
Revolver						
Rope						
Lead Pipe						
Wrench						
ROOMS						
Hall						
Lounge						
Dining Room						
Kitchen						
Ball Room						
Conservatory						
Billard Room						
Library						
Study						

CLUE SCORE SHEET

SUSPECTS					
Col. Mustard					
Prof. Plum					
Mr. Green					
Mrs. Peacock					
Miss Scarlett					
Mrs. White					
WEAPONS					
Knife					
Candlestick					
Revolver					
Rope					
Lead Pipe					
Wrench					
ROOMS					
Hall					
Lounge					
Dining Room					
Kitchen					
Ball Room					
Conservatory					
Billard Room					
Library					
Study					

CLUE SCORE SHEET

SUSPECTS						
Col. Mustard						
Prof. Plum						
Mr. Green						
Mrs. Peacock						
Miss Scarlett						
Mrs. White						
WEAPONS						
Knife						
Candlestick						
Revolver						
Rope						
Lead Pipe						
Wrench						
ROOMS						
Hall						
Lounge						
Dining Room						
Kitchen						
Ball Room						
Conservatory						
Billard Room						
Library						
Study						

CLUE SCORE SHEET

SUSPECTS						
Col. Mustard						
Prof. Plum						
Mr. Green						
Mrs. Peacock						
Miss Scarlett						
Mrs. White						
WEAPONS						
Knife						
Candlestick						
Revolver						
Rope						
Lead Pipe						
Wrench						
ROOMS						
Hall						
Lounge						
Dining Room						
Kitchen						
Ball Room						
Conservatory						
Billard Room						
Library						
Study						

CLUE SCORE SHEET

SUSPECTS						
Col. Mustard						
Prof. Plum						
Mr. Green						
Mrs. Peacock						
Miss Scarlett						
Mrs. White						
WEAPONS						
Knife						
Candlestick						
Revolver						
Rope						
Lead Pipe						
Wrench						
ROOMS						
Hall						
Lounge						
Dining Room						
Kitchen						
Ball Room						
Conservatory						
Billard Room						
Library						
Study						

CLUE SCORE SHEET

SUSPECTS						
Col. Mustard						
Prof. Plum						
Mr. Green						
Mrs. Peacock						
Miss Scarlett						
Mrs. White						
WEAPONS						
Knife						
Candlestick						
Revolver						
Rope						
Lead Pipe						
Wrench						
ROOMS						
Hall						
Lounge						
Dining Room						
Kitchen						
Ball Room						
Conservatory						
Billard Room						
Library						
Study						

CLUE SCORE SHEET

SUSPECTS					
Col. Mustard					
Prof. Plum					
Mr. Green					
Mrs. Peacock					
Miss Scarlett					
Mrs. White					
WEAPONS					
Knife					
Candlestick					
Revolver					
Rope					
Lead Pipe					
Wrench					
ROOMS					
Hall					
Lounge					
Dining Room					
Kitchen					
Ball Room					
Conservatory					
Billard Room					
Library					
Study					

CLUE SCORE SHEET

SUSPECTS					
Col. Mustard					
Prof. Plum					
Mr. Green					
Mrs. Peacock					
Miss Scarlett					
Mrs. White					
WEAPONS					
Knife					
Candlestick					
Revolver					
Rope					
Lead Pipe					
Wrench					
ROOMS					
Hall					
Lounge					
Dining Room					
Kitchen					
Ball Room					
Conservatory					
Billard Room					
Library					
Study					

CLUE SCORE SHEET

SUSPECTS						
Col. Mustard						
Prof. Plum						
Mr. Green						
Mrs. Peacock						
Miss Scarlett						
Mrs. White						
WEAPONS						
Knife						
Candlestick						
Revolver						
Rope						
Lead Pipe						
Wrench						
ROOMS						
Hall						
Lounge						
Dining Room						
Kitchen						
Ball Room						
Conservatory						
Billard Room						
Library						
Study						

CLUE SCORE SHEET

SUSPECTS						
Col. Mustard						
Prof. Plum						
Mr. Green						
Mrs. Peacock						
Miss Scarlett						
Mrs. White						
WEAPONS						
Knife						
Candlestick						
Revolver						
Rope						
Lead Pipe						
Wrench						
ROOMS						
Hall						
Lounge						
Dining Room						
Kitchen						
Ball Room						
Conservatory						
Billard Room						
Library						
Study						

CLUE SCORE SHEET

SUSPECTS					
Col. Mustard					
Prof. Plum					
Mr. Green					
Mrs. Peacock					
Miss Scarlett					
Mrs. White					
WEAPONS					
Knife					
Candlestick					
Revolver					
Rope					
Lead Pipe					
Wrench					
ROOMS					
Hall					
Lounge					
Dining Room					
Kitchen					
Ball Room					
Conservatory					
Billard Room					
Library					
Study					

CLUE SCORE SHEET

SUSPECTS						
Col. Mustard						
Prof. Plum						
Mr. Green						
Mrs. Peacock						
Miss Scarlett						
Mrs. White						
WEAPONS						
Knife						
Candlestick						
Revolver						
Rope						
Lead Pipe						
Wrench						
ROOMS						
Hall						
Lounge						
Dining Room						
Kitchen						
Ball Room						
Conservatory						
Billard Room						
Library						
Study						

CLUE SCORE SHEET

SUSPECTS					
Col. Mustard					
Prof. Plum					
Mr. Green					
Mrs. Peacock					
Miss Scarlett					
Mrs. White					
WEAPONS					
Knife					
Candlestick					
Revolver					
Rope					
Lead Pipe					
Wrench					
ROOMS					
Hall					
Lounge					
Dining Room					
Kitchen					
Ball Room					
Conservatory					
Billard Room					
Library					
Study					

CLUE SCORE SHEET

SUSPECTS					
Col. Mustard					
Prof. Plum					
Mr. Green					
Mrs. Peacock					
Miss Scarlett					
Mrs. White					
WEAPONS					
Knife					
Candlestick					
Revolver					
Rope					
Lead Pipe					
Wrench					
ROOMS					
Hall					
Lounge					
Dining Room					
Kitchen					
Ball Room					
Conservatory					
Billard Room					
Library					
Study					

CLUE SCORE SHEET

SUSPECTS						
Col. Mustard						
Prof. Plum						
Mr. Green						
Mrs. Peacock						
Miss Scarlett						
Mrs. White						
WEAPONS						
Knife						
Candlestick						
Revolver						
Rope						
Lead Pipe						
Wrench						
ROOMS						
Hall						
Lounge						
Dining Room						
Kitchen						
Ball Room						
Conservatory						
Billard Room						
Library						
Study						

CLUE SCORE SHEET

SUSPECTS						
Col. Mustard						
Prof. Plum						
Mr. Green						
Mrs. Peacock						
Miss Scarlett						
Mrs. White						
WEAPONS						
Knife						
Candlestick						
Revolver						
Rope						
Lead Pipe						
Wrench						
ROOMS						
Hall						
Lounge						
Dining Room						
Kitchen						
Ball Room						
Conservatory						
Billard Room						
Library						
Study						

CLUE SCORE SHEET

SUSPECTS					
Col. Mustard					
Prof. Plum					
Mr. Green					
Mrs. Peacock					
Miss Scarlett					
Mrs. White					
WEAPONS					
Knife					
Candlestick					
Revolver					
Rope					
Lead Pipe					
Wrench					
ROOMS					
Hall					
Lounge					
Dining Room					
Kitchen					
Ball Room					
Conservatory					
Billard Room					
Library					
Study					

CLUE SCORE SHEET

SUSPECTS						
Col. Mustard						
Prof. Plum						
Mr. Green						
Mrs. Peacock						
Miss Scarlett						
Mrs. White						
WEAPONS						
Knife						
Candlestick						
Revolver						
Rope						
Lead Pipe						
Wrench						
ROOMS						
Hall						
Lounge						
Dining Room						
Kitchen						
Ball Room						
Conservatory						
Billard Room						
Library						
Study						

CLUE SCORE SHEET

SUSPECTS						
Col. Mustard						
Prof. Plum						
Mr. Green						
Mrs. Peacock						
Miss Scarlett						
Mrs. White						
WEAPONS						
Knife						
Candlestick						
Revolver						
Rope						
Lead Pipe						
Wrench						
ROOMS						
Hall						
Lounge						
Dining Room						
Kitchen						
Ball Room						
Conservatory						
Billard Room						
Library						
Study						

CLUE SCORE SHEET

SUSPECTS						
Col. Mustard						
Prof. Plum						
Mr. Green						
Mrs. Peacock						
Miss Scarlett						
Mrs. White						
WEAPONS						
Knife						
Candlestick						
Revolver						
Rope						
Lead Pipe						
Wrench						
ROOMS						
Hall						
Lounge						
Dining Room						
Kitchen						
Ball Room						
Conservatory						
Billard Room						
Library						
Study						

CLUE SCORE SHEET

SUSPECTS					
Col. Mustard					
Prof. Plum					
Mr. Green					
Mrs. Peacock					
Miss Scarlett					
Mrs. White					
WEAPONS					
Knife					
Candlestick					
Revolver					
Rope					
Lead Pipe					
Wrench					
ROOMS					
Hall					
Lounge					
Dining Room					
Kitchen					
Ball Room					
Conservatory					
Billard Room					
Library					
Study					

CLUE SCORE SHEET

SUSPECTS					
Col. Mustard					
Prof. Plum					
Mr. Green					
Mrs. Peacock					
Miss Scarlett					
Mrs. White					
WEAPONS					
Knife					
Candlestick					
Revolver					
Rope					
Lead Pipe					
Wrench					
ROOMS					
Hall					
Lounge					
Dining Room					
Kitchen					
Ball Room					
Conservatory					
Billard Room					
Library					
Study					

CLUE SCORE SHEET

SUSPECTS						
Col. Mustard						
Prof. Plum						
Mr. Green						
Mrs. Peacock						
Miss Scarlett						
Mrs. White						
WEAPONS						
Knife						
Candlestick						
Revolver						
Rope						
Lead Pipe						
Wrench						
ROOMS						
Hall						
Lounge						
Dining Room						
Kitchen						
Ball Room						
Conservatory						
Billard Room						
Library						
Study						

CLUE SCORE SHEET

SUSPECTS						
Col. Mustard						
Prof. Plum						
Mr. Green						
Mrs. Peacock						
Miss Scarlett						
Mrs. White						
WEAPONS						
Knife						
Candlestick						
Revolver						
Rope						
Lead Pipe						
Wrench						
ROOMS						
Hall						
Lounge						
Dining Room						
Kitchen						
Ball Room						
Conservatory						
Billard Room						
Library						
Study						

CLUE SCORE SHEET

SUSPECTS					
Col. Mustard					
Prof. Plum					
Mr. Green					
Mrs. Peacock					
Miss Scarlett					
Mrs. White					
WEAPONS					
Knife					
Candlestick					
Revolver					
Rope					
Lead Pipe					
Wrench					
ROOMS					
Hall					
Lounge					
Dining Room					
Kitchen					
Ball Room					
Conservatory					
Billard Room					
Library					
Study					

CLUE SCORE SHEET

SUSPECTS						
Col. Mustard						
Prof. Plum						
Mr. Green						
Mrs. Peacock						
Miss Scarlett						
Mrs. White						
WEAPONS						
Knife						
Candlestick						
Revolver						
Rope						
Lead Pipe						
Wrench						
ROOMS						
Hall						
Lounge						
Dining Room						
Kitchen						
Ball Room						
Conservatory						
Billard Room						
Library						
Study						

CLUE SCORE SHEET

SUSPECTS					
Col. Mustard					
Prof. Plum					
Mr. Green					
Mrs. Peacock					
Miss Scarlett					
Mrs. White					

WEAPONS					
Knife					
Candlestick					
Revolver					
Rope					
Lead Pipe					
Wrench					

ROOMS					
Hall					
Lounge					
Dining Room					
Kitchen					
Ball Room					
Conservatory					
Billard Room					
Library					
Study					

CLUE SCORE SHEET

SUSPECTS					
Col. Mustard					
Prof. Plum					
Mr. Green					
Mrs. Peacock					
Miss Scarlett					
Mrs. White					
WEAPONS					
Knife					
Candlestick					
Revolver					
Rope					
Lead Pipe					
Wrench					
ROOMS					
Hall					
Lounge					
Dining Room					
Kitchen					
Ball Room					
Conservatory					
Billard Room					
Library					
Study					

CLUE SCORE SHEET

SUSPECTS					
Col. Mustard					
Prof. Plum					
Mr. Green					
Mrs. Peacock					
Miss Scarlett					
Mrs. White					
WEAPONS					
Knife					
Candlestick					
Revolver					
Rope					
Lead Pipe					
Wrench					
ROOMS					
Hall					
Lounge					
Dining Room					
Kitchen					
Ball Room					
Conservatory					
Billard Room					
Library					
Study					

CLUE SCORE SHEET

SUSPECTS						
Col. Mustard						
Prof. Plum						
Mr. Green						
Mrs. Peacock						
Miss Scarlett						
Mrs. White						
WEAPONS						
Knife						
Candlestick						
Revolver						
Rope						
Lead Pipe						
Wrench						
ROOMS						
Hall						
Lounge						
Dining Room						
Kitchen						
Ball Room						
Conservatory						
Billard Room						
Library						
Study						

CLUE SCORE SHEET

SUSPECTS						
Col. Mustard						
Prof. Plum						
Mr. Green						
Mrs. Peacock						
Miss Scarlett						
Mrs. White						
WEAPONS						
Knife						
Candlestick						
Revolver						
Rope						
Lead Pipe						
Wrench						
ROOMS						
Hall						
Lounge						
Dining Room						
Kitchen						
Ball Room						
Conservatory						
Billard Room						
Library						
Study						

CLUE SCORE SHEET

SUSPECTS					
Col. Mustard					
Prof. Plum					
Mr. Green					
Mrs. Peacock					
Miss Scarlett					
Mrs. White					
WEAPONS					
Knife					
Candlestick					
Revolver					
Rope					
Lead Pipe					
Wrench					
ROOMS					
Hall					
Lounge					
Dining Room					
Kitchen					
Ball Room					
Conservatory					
Billard Room					
Library					
Study					

CLUE SCORE SHEET

SUSPECTS						
Col. Mustard						
Prof. Plum						
Mr. Green						
Mrs. Peacock						
Miss Scarlett						
Mrs. White						
WEAPONS						
Knife						
Candlestick						
Revolver						
Rope						
Lead Pipe						
Wrench						
ROOMS						
Hall						
Lounge						
Dining Room						
Kitchen						
Ball Room						
Conservatory						
Billard Room						
Library						
Study						

CLUE SCORE SHEET

SUSPECTS						
Col. Mustard						
Prof. Plum						
Mr. Green						
Mrs. Peacock						
Miss Scarlett						
Mrs. White						
WEAPONS						
Knife						
Candlestick						
Revolver						
Rope						
Lead Pipe						
Wrench						
ROOMS						
Hall						
Lounge						
Dining Room						
Kitchen						
Ball Room						
Conservatory						
Billard Room						
Library						
Study						

CLUE SCORE SHEET

SUSPECTS					
Col. Mustard					
Prof. Plum					
Mr. Green					
Mrs. Peacock					
Miss Scarlett					
Mrs. White					
WEAPONS					
Knife					
Candlestick					
Revolver					
Rope					
Lead Pipe					
Wrench					
ROOMS					
Hall					
Lounge					
Dining Room					
Kitchen					
Ball Room					
Conservatory					
Billard Room					
Library					
Study					

CLUE SCORE SHEET

SUSPECTS						
Col. Mustard						
Prof. Plum						
Mr. Green						
Mrs. Peacock						
Miss Scarlett						
Mrs. White						
WEAPONS						
Knife						
Candlestick						
Revolver						
Rope						
Lead Pipe						
Wrench						
ROOMS						
Hall						
Lounge						
Dining Room						
Kitchen						
Ball Room						
Conservatory						
Billard Room						
Library						
Study						

CLUE SCORE SHEET

SUSPECTS						
Col. Mustard						
Prof. Plum						
Mr. Green						
Mrs. Peacock						
Miss Scarlett						
Mrs. White						
WEAPONS						
Knife						
Candlestick						
Revolver						
Rope						
Lead Pipe						
Wrench						
ROOMS						
Hall						
Lounge						
Dining Room						
Kitchen						
Ball Room						
Conservatory						
Billard Room						
Library						
Study						

CLUE SCORE SHEET

SUSPECTS						
Col. Mustard						
Prof. Plum						
Mr. Green						
Mrs. Peacock						
Miss Scarlett						
Mrs. White						
WEAPONS						
Knife						
Candlestick						
Revolver						
Rope						
Lead Pipe						
Wrench						
ROOMS						
Hall						
Lounge						
Dining Room						
Kitchen						
Ball Room						
Conservatory						
Billard Room						
Library						
Study						

CLUE SCORE SHEET

SUSPECTS					
Col. Mustard					
Prof. Plum					
Mr. Green					
Mrs. Peacock					
Miss Scarlett					
Mrs. White					
WEAPONS					
Knife					
Candlestick					
Revolver					
Rope					
Lead Pipe					
Wrench					
ROOMS					
Hall					
Lounge					
Dining Room					
Kitchen					
Ball Room					
Conservatory					
Billard Room					
Library					
Study					

CLUE SCORE SHEET

SUSPECTS						
Col. Mustard						
Prof. Plum						
Mr. Green						
Mrs. Peacock						
Miss Scarlett						
Mrs. White						
WEAPONS						
Knife						
Candlestick						
Revolver						
Rope						
Lead Pipe						
Wrench						
ROOMS						
Hall						
Lounge						
Dining Room						
Kitchen						
Ball Room						
Conservatory						
Billard Room						
Library						
Study						

CLUE SCORE SHEET

SUSPECTS						
Col. Mustard						
Prof. Plum						
Mr. Green						
Mrs. Peacock						
Miss Scarlett						
Mrs. White						
WEAPONS						
Knife						
Candlestick						
Revolver						
Rope						
Lead Pipe						
Wrench						
ROOMS						
Hall						
Lounge						
Dining Room						
Kitchen						
Ball Room						
Conservatory						
Billard Room						
Library						
Study						

CLUE SCORE SHEET

SUSPECTS					
Col. Mustard					
Prof. Plum					
Mr. Green					
Mrs. Peacock					
Miss Scarlett					
Mrs. White					
WEAPONS					
Knife					
Candlestick					
Revolver					
Rope					
Lead Pipe					
Wrench					
ROOMS					
Hall					
Lounge					
Dining Room					
Kitchen					
Ball Room					
Conservatory					
Billard Room					
Library					
Study					

CLUE SCORE SHEET

SUSPECTS						
Col. Mustard						
Prof. Plum						
Mr. Green						
Mrs. Peacock						
Miss Scarlett						
Mrs. White						
WEAPONS						
Knife						
Candlestick						
Revolver						
Rope						
Lead Pipe						
Wrench						
ROOMS						
Hall						
Lounge						
Dining Room						
Kitchen						
Ball Room						
Conservatory						
Billard Room						
Library						
Study						

CLUE SCORE SHEET

SUSPECTS					
Col. Mustard					
Prof. Plum					
Mr. Green					
Mrs. Peacock					
Miss Scarlett					
Mrs. White					
WEAPONS					
Knife					
Candlestick					
Revolver					
Rope					
Lead Pipe					
Wrench					
ROOMS					
Hall					
Lounge					
Dining Room					
Kitchen					
Ball Room					
Conservatory					
Billard Room					
Library					
Study					

CLUE SCORE SHEET

SUSPECTS						
Col. Mustard						
Prof. Plum						
Mr. Green						
Mrs. Peacock						
Miss Scarlett						
Mrs. White						
WEAPONS						
Knife						
Candlestick						
Revolver						
Rope						
Lead Pipe						
Wrench						
ROOMS						
Hall						
Lounge						
Dining Room						
Kitchen						
Ball Room						
Conservatory						
Billard Room						
Library						
Study						

CLUE SCORE SHEET

SUSPECTS						
Col. Mustard						
Prof. Plum						
Mr. Green						
Mrs. Peacock						
Miss Scarlett						
Mrs. White						
WEAPONS						
Knife						
Candlestick						
Revolver						
Rope						
Lead Pipe						
Wrench						
ROOMS						
Hall						
Lounge						
Dining Room						
Kitchen						
Ball Room						
Conservatory						
Billard Room						
Library						
Study						

CLUE SCORE SHEET

SUSPECTS						
Col. Mustard						
Prof. Plum						
Mr. Green						
Mrs. Peacock						
Miss Scarlett						
Mrs. White						
WEAPONS						
Knife						
Candlestick						
Revolver						
Rope						
Lead Pipe						
Wrench						
ROOMS						
Hall						
Lounge						
Dining Room						
Kitchen						
Ball Room						
Conservatory						
Billard Room						
Library						
Study						

CLUE SCORE SHEET

SUSPECTS					
Col. Mustard					
Prof. Plum					
Mr. Green					
Mrs. Peacock					
Miss Scarlett					
Mrs. White					
WEAPONS					
Knife					
Candlestick					
Revolver					
Rope					
Lead Pipe					
Wrench					
ROOMS					
Hall					
Lounge					
Dining Room					
Kitchen					
Ball Room					
Conservatory					
Billard Room					
Library					
Study					

CLUE SCORE SHEET

SUSPECTS					
Col. Mustard					
Prof. Plum					
Mr. Green					
Mrs. Peacock					
Miss Scarlett					
Mrs. White					
WEAPONS					
Knife					
Candlestick					
Revolver					
Rope					
Lead Pipe					
Wrench					
ROOMS					
Hall					
Lounge					
Dining Room					
Kitchen					
Ball Room					
Conservatory					
Billard Room					
Library					
Study					

CLUE SCORE SHEET

SUSPECTS					
Col. Mustard					
Prof. Plum					
Mr. Green					
Mrs. Peacock					
Miss Scarlett					
Mrs. White					
WEAPONS					
Knife					
Candlestick					
Revolver					
Rope					
Lead Pipe					
Wrench					
ROOMS					
Hall					
Lounge					
Dining Room					
Kitchen					
Ball Room					
Conservatory					
Billard Room					
Library					
Study					

CLUE SCORE SHEET

SUSPECTS					
Col. Mustard					
Prof. Plum					
Mr. Green					
Mrs. Peacock					
Miss Scarlett					
Mrs. White					
WEAPONS					
Knife					
Candlestick					
Revolver					
Rope					
Lead Pipe					
Wrench					
ROOMS					
Hall					
Lounge					
Dining Room					
Kitchen					
Ball Room					
Conservatory					
Billard Room					
Library					
Study					

CLUE SCORE SHEET

SUSPECTS					
Col. Mustard					
Prof. Plum					
Mr. Green					
Mrs. Peacock					
Miss Scarlett					
Mrs. White					
WEAPONS					
Knife					
Candlestick					
Revolver					
Rope					
Lead Pipe					
Wrench					
ROOMS					
Hall					
Lounge					
Dining Room					
Kitchen					
Ball Room					
Conservatory					
Billard Room					
Library					
Study					

CLUE SCORE SHEET

SUSPECTS					
Col. Mustard					
Prof. Plum					
Mr. Green					
Mrs. Peacock					
Miss Scarlett					
Mrs. White					
WEAPONS					
Knife					
Candlestick					
Revolver					
Rope					
Lead Pipe					
Wrench					
ROOMS					
Hall					
Lounge					
Dining Room					
Kitchen					
Ball Room					
Conservatory					
Billard Room					
Library					
Study					

CLUE SCORE SHEET

SUSPECTS					
Col. Mustard					
Prof. Plum					
Mr. Green					
Mrs. Peacock					
Miss Scarlett					
Mrs. White					
WEAPONS					
Knife					
Candlestick					
Revolver					
Rope					
Lead Pipe					
Wrench					
ROOMS					
Hall					
Lounge					
Dining Room					
Kitchen					
Ball Room					
Conservatory					
Billard Room					
Library					
Study					

CLUE SCORE SHEET

SUSPECTS						
Col. Mustard						
Prof. Plum						
Mr. Green						
Mrs. Peacock						
Miss Scarlett						
Mrs. White						
WEAPONS						
Knife						
Candlestick						
Revolver						
Rope						
Lead Pipe						
Wrench						
ROOMS						
Hall						
Lounge						
Dining Room						
Kitchen						
Ball Room						
Conservatory						
Billard Room						
Library						
Study						

CLUE SCORE SHEET

SUSPECTS						
Col. Mustard						
Prof. Plum						
Mr. Green						
Mrs. Peacock						
Miss Scarlett						
Mrs. White						
WEAPONS						
Knife						
Candlestick						
Revolver						
Rope						
Lead Pipe						
Wrench						
ROOMS						
Hall						
Lounge						
Dining Room						
Kitchen						
Ball Room						
Conservatory						
Billard Room						
Library						
Study						

CLUE SCORE SHEET

SUSPECTS						
Col. Mustard						
Prof. Plum						
Mr. Green						
Mrs. Peacock						
Miss Scarlett						
Mrs. White						
WEAPONS						
Knife						
Candlestick						
Revolver						
Rope						
Lead Pipe						
Wrench						
ROOMS						
Hall						
Lounge						
Dining Room						
Kitchen						
Ball Room						
Conservatory						
Billard Room						
Library						
Study						

CLUE SCORE SHEET

SUSPECTS						
Col. Mustard						
Prof. Plum						
Mr. Green						
Mrs. Peacock						
Miss Scarlett						
Mrs. White						
WEAPONS						
Knife						
Candlestick						
Revolver						
Rope						
Lead Pipe						
Wrench						
ROOMS						
Hall						
Lounge						
Dining Room						
Kitchen						
Ball Room						
Conservatory						
Billard Room						
Library						
Study						

CLUE SCORE SHEET

SUSPECTS						
Col. Mustard						
Prof. Plum						
Mr. Green						
Mrs. Peacock						
Miss Scarlett						
Mrs. White						
WEAPONS						
Knife						
Candlestick						
Revolver						
Rope						
Lead Pipe						
Wrench						
ROOMS						
Hall						
Lounge						
Dining Room						
Kitchen						
Ball Room						
Conservatory						
Billard Room						
Library						
Study						

CLUE SCORE SHEET

SUSPECTS					
Col. Mustard					
Prof. Plum					
Mr. Green					
Mrs. Peacock					
Miss Scarlett					
Mrs. White					
WEAPONS					
Knife					
Candlestick					
Revolver					
Rope					
Lead Pipe					
Wrench					
ROOMS					
Hall					
Lounge					
Dining Room					
Kitchen					
Ball Room					
Conservatory					
Billard Room					
Library					
Study					

CLUE SCORE SHEET

SUSPECTS						
Col. Mustard						
Prof. Plum						
Mr. Green						
Mrs. Peacock						
Miss Scarlett						
Mrs. White						
WEAPONS						
Knife						
Candlestick						
Revolver						
Rope						
Lead Pipe						
Wrench						
ROOMS						
Hall						
Lounge						
Dining Room						
Kitchen						
Ball Room						
Conservatory						
Billard Room						
Library						
Study						

CLUE SCORE SHEET

SUSPECTS					
Col. Mustard					
Prof. Plum					
Mr. Green					
Mrs. Peacock					
Miss Scarlett					
Mrs. White					
WEAPONS					
Knife					
Candlestick					
Revolver					
Rope					
Lead Pipe					
Wrench					
ROOMS					
Hall					
Lounge					
Dining Room					
Kitchen					
Ball Room					
Conservatory					
Billard Room					
Library					
Study					

CLUE SCORE SHEET

SUSPECTS						
Col. Mustard						
Prof. Plum						
Mr. Green						
Mrs. Peacock						
Miss Scarlett						
Mrs. White						
WEAPONS						
Knife						
Candlestick						
Revolver						
Rope						
Lead Pipe						
Wrench						
ROOMS						
Hall						
Lounge						
Dining Room						
Kitchen						
Ball Room						
Conservatory						
Billard Room						
Library						
Study						

CLUE SCORE SHEET

SUSPECTS					
Col. Mustard					
Prof. Plum					
Mr. Green					
Mrs. Peacock					
Miss Scarlett					
Mrs. White					
WEAPONS					
Knife					
Candlestick					
Revolver					
Rope					
Lead Pipe					
Wrench					
ROOMS					
Hall					
Lounge					
Dining Room					
Kitchen					
Ball Room					
Conservatory					
Billard Room					
Library					
Study					

CLUE SCORE SHEET

SUSPECTS					
Col. Mustard					
Prof. Plum					
Mr. Green					
Mrs. Peacock					
Miss Scarlett					
Mrs. White					
WEAPONS					
Knife					
Candlestick					
Revolver					
Rope					
Lead Pipe					
Wrench					
ROOMS					
Hall					
Lounge					
Dining Room					
Kitchen					
Ball Room					
Conservatory					
Billard Room					
Library					
Study					

CLUE SCORE SHEET

SUSPECTS					
Col. Mustard					
Prof. Plum					
Mr. Green					
Mrs. Peacock					
Miss Scarlett					
Mrs. White					
WEAPONS					
Knife					
Candlestick					
Revolver					
Rope					
Lead Pipe					
Wrench					
ROOMS					
Hall					
Lounge					
Dining Room					
Kitchen					
Ball Room					
Conservatory					
Billard Room					
Library					
Study					

CLUE SCORE SHEET

SUSPECTS						
Col. Mustard						
Prof. Plum						
Mr. Green						
Mrs. Peacock						
Miss Scarlett						
Mrs. White						
WEAPONS						
Knife						
Candlestick						
Revolver						
Rope						
Lead Pipe						
Wrench						
ROOMS						
Hall						
Lounge						
Dining Room						
Kitchen						
Ball Room						
Conservatory						
Billard Room						
Library						
Study						

CLUE SCORE SHEET

SUSPECTS					
Col. Mustard					
Prof. Plum					
Mr. Green					
Mrs. Peacock					
Miss Scarlett					
Mrs. White					
WEAPONS					
Knife					
Candlestick					
Revolver					
Rope					
Lead Pipe					
Wrench					
ROOMS					
Hall					
Lounge					
Dining Room					
Kitchen					
Ball Room					
Conservatory					
Billard Room					
Library					
Study					

CLUE SCORE SHEET

SUSPECTS						
Col. Mustard						
Prof. Plum						
Mr. Green						
Mrs. Peacock						
Miss Scarlett						
Mrs. White						
WEAPONS						
Knife						
Candlestick						
Revolver						
Rope						
Lead Pipe						
Wrench						
ROOMS						
Hall						
Lounge						
Dining Room						
Kitchen						
Ball Room						
Conservatory						
Billard Room						
Library						
Study						

CLUE SCORE SHEET

SUSPECTS					
Col. Mustard					
Prof. Plum					
Mr. Green					
Mrs. Peacock					
Miss Scarlett					
Mrs. White					
WEAPONS					
Knife					
Candlestick					
Revolver					
Rope					
Lead Pipe					
Wrench					
ROOMS					
Hall					
Lounge					
Dining Room					
Kitchen					
Ball Room					
Conservatory					
Billard Room					
Library					
Study					

CLUE SCORE SHEET

SUSPECTS						
Col. Mustard						
Prof. Plum						
Mr. Green						
Mrs. Peacock						
Miss Scarlett						
Mrs. White						
WEAPONS						
Knife						
Candlestick						
Revolver						
Rope						
Lead Pipe						
Wrench						
ROOMS						
Hall						
Lounge						
Dining Room						
Kitchen						
Ball Room						
Conservatory						
Billard Room						
Library						
Study						

CLUE SCORE SHEET

SUSPECTS					
Col. Mustard					
Prof. Plum					
Mr. Green					
Mrs. Peacock					
Miss Scarlett					
Mrs. White					
WEAPONS					
Knife					
Candlestick					
Revolver					
Rope					
Lead Pipe					
Wrench					
ROOMS					
Hall					
Lounge					
Dining Room					
Kitchen					
Ball Room					
Conservatory					
Billard Room					
Library					
Study					

CLUE SCORE SHEET

SUSPECTS						
Col. Mustard						
Prof. Plum						
Mr. Green						
Mrs. Peacock						
Miss Scarlett						
Mrs. White						
WEAPONS						
Knife						
Candlestick						
Revolver						
Rope						
Lead Pipe						
Wrench						
ROOMS						
Hall						
Lounge						
Dining Room						
Kitchen						
Ball Room						
Conservatory						
Billard Room						
Library						
Study						

CLUE SCORE SHEET

SUSPECTS					
Col. Mustard					
Prof. Plum					
Mr. Green					
Mrs. Peacock					
Miss Scarlett					
Mrs. White					
WEAPONS					
Knife					
Candlestick					
Revolver					
Rope					
Lead Pipe					
Wrench					
ROOMS					
Hall					
Lounge					
Dining Room					
Kitchen					
Ball Room					
Conservatory					
Billard Room					
Library					
Study					

CLUE SCORE SHEET

SUSPECTS						
Col. Mustard						
Prof. Plum						
Mr. Green						
Mrs. Peacock						
Miss Scarlett						
Mrs. White						
WEAPONS						
Knife						
Candlestick						
Revolver						
Rope						
Lead Pipe						
Wrench						
ROOMS						
Hall						
Lounge						
Dining Room						
Kitchen						
Ball Room						
Conservatory						
Billard Room						
Library						
Study						

CLUE SCORE SHEET

SUSPECTS					
Col. Mustard					
Prof. Plum					
Mr. Green					
Mrs. Peacock					
Miss Scarlett					
Mrs. White					
WEAPONS					
Knife					
Candlestick					
Revolver					
Rope					
Lead Pipe					
Wrench					
ROOMS					
Hall					
Lounge					
Dining Room					
Kitchen					
Ball Room					
Conservatory					
Billard Room					
Library					
Study					

CLUE SCORE SHEET

SUSPECTS					
Col. Mustard					
Prof. Plum					
Mr. Green					
Mrs. Peacock					
Miss Scarlett					
Mrs. White					
WEAPONS					
Knife					
Candlestick					
Revolver					
Rope					
Lead Pipe					
Wrench					
ROOMS					
Hall					
Lounge					
Dining Room					
Kitchen					
Ball Room					
Conservatory					
Billard Room					
Library					
Study					

CLUE SCORE SHEET

SUSPECTS					
Col. Mustard					
Prof. Plum					
Mr. Green					
Mrs. Peacock					
Miss Scarlett					
Mrs. White					
WEAPONS					
Knife					
Candlestick					
Revolver					
Rope					
Lead Pipe					
Wrench					
ROOMS					
Hall					
Lounge					
Dining Room					
Kitchen					
Ball Room					
Conservatory					
Billard Room					
Library					
Study					

CLUE SCORE SHEET

SUSPECTS						
Col. Mustard						
Prof. Plum						
Mr. Green						
Mrs. Peacock						
Miss Scarlett						
Mrs. White						
WEAPONS						
Knife						
Candlestick						
Revolver						
Rope						
Lead Pipe						
Wrench						
ROOMS						
Hall						
Lounge						
Dining Room						
Kitchen						
Ball Room						
Conservatory						
Billard Room						
Library						
Study						

CLUE SCORE SHEET

SUSPECTS					
Col. Mustard					
Prof. Plum					
Mr. Green					
Mrs. Peacock					
Miss Scarlett					
Mrs. White					
WEAPONS					
Knife					
Candlestick					
Revolver					
Rope					
Lead Pipe					
Wrench					
ROOMS					
Hall					
Lounge					
Dining Room					
Kitchen					
Ball Room					
Conservatory					
Billard Room					
Library					
Study					

CLUE SCORE SHEET

SUSPECTS						
Col. Mustard						
Prof. Plum						
Mr. Green						
Mrs. Peacock						
Miss Scarlett						
Mrs. White						
WEAPONS						
Knife						
Candlestick						
Revolver						
Rope						
Lead Pipe						
Wrench						
ROOMS						
Hall						
Lounge						
Dining Room						
Kitchen						
Ball Room						
Conservatory						
Billard Room						
Library						
Study						

CLUE SCORE SHEET

SUSPECTS					
Col. Mustard					
Prof. Plum					
Mr. Green					
Mrs. Peacock					
Miss Scarlett					
Mrs. White					
WEAPONS					
Knife					
Candlestick					
Revolver					
Rope					
Lead Pipe					
Wrench					
ROOMS					
Hall					
Lounge					
Dining Room					
Kitchen					
Ball Room					
Conservatory					
Billard Room					
Library					
Study					

CLUE SCORE SHEET

SUSPECTS					
Col. Mustard					
Prof. Plum					
Mr. Green					
Mrs. Peacock					
Miss Scarlett					
Mrs. White					
WEAPONS					
Knife					
Candlestick					
Revolver					
Rope					
Lead Pipe					
Wrench					
ROOMS					
Hall					
Lounge					
Dining Room					
Kitchen					
Ball Room					
Conservatory					
Billard Room					
Library					
Study					

CLUE SCORE SHEET

SUSPECTS					
Col. Mustard					
Prof. Plum					
Mr. Green					
Mrs. Peacock					
Miss Scarlett					
Mrs. White					
WEAPONS					
Knife					
Candlestick					
Revolver					
Rope					
Lead Pipe					
Wrench					
ROOMS					
Hall					
Lounge					
Dining Room					
Kitchen					
Ball Room					
Conservatory					
Billard Room					
Library					
Study					

CLUE SCORE SHEET

SUSPECTS					
Col. Mustard					
Prof. Plum					
Mr. Green					
Mrs. Peacock					
Miss Scarlett					
Mrs. White					
WEAPONS					
Knife					
Candlestick					
Revolver					
Rope					
Lead Pipe					
Wrench					
ROOMS					
Hall					
Lounge					
Dining Room					
Kitchen					
Ball Room					
Conservatory					
Billard Room					
Library					
Study					

CLUE SCORE SHEET

SUSPECTS					
Col. Mustard					
Prof. Plum					
Mr. Green					
Mrs. Peacock					
Miss Scarlett					
Mrs. White					
WEAPONS					
Knife					
Candlestick					
Revolver					
Rope					
Lead Pipe					
Wrench					
ROOMS					
Hall					
Lounge					
Dining Room					
Kitchen					
Ball Room					
Conservatory					
Billard Room					
Library					
Study					

CLUE SCORE SHEET

SUSPECTS						
Col. Mustard						
Prof. Plum						
Mr. Green						
Mrs. Peacock						
Miss Scarlett						
Mrs. White						
WEAPONS						
Knife						
Candlestick						
Revolver						
Rope						
Lead Pipe						
Wrench						
ROOMS						
Hall						
Lounge						
Dining Room						
Kitchen						
Ball Room						
Conservatory						
Billard Room						
Library						
Study						

CLUE SCORE SHEET

SUSPECTS						
Col. Mustard						
Prof. Plum						
Mr. Green						
Mrs. Peacock						
Miss Scarlett						
Mrs. White						
WEAPONS						
Knife						
Candlestick						
Revolver						
Rope						
Lead Pipe						
Wrench						
ROOMS						
Hall						
Lounge						
Dining Room						
Kitchen						
Ball Room						
Conservatory						
Billard Room						
Library						
Study						

CLUE SCORE SHEET

SUSPECTS						
Col. Mustard						
Prof. Plum						
Mr. Green						
Mrs. Peacock						
Miss Scarlett						
Mrs. White						
WEAPONS						
Knife						
Candlestick						
Revolver						
Rope						
Lead Pipe						
Wrench						
ROOMS						
Hall						
Lounge						
Dining Room						
Kitchen						
Ball Room						
Conservatory						
Billard Room						
Library						
Study						

CLUE SCORE SHEET

SUSPECTS						
Col. Mustard						
Prof. Plum						
Mr. Green						
Mrs. Peacock						
Miss Scarlett						
Mrs. White						
WEAPONS						
Knife						
Candlestick						
Revolver						
Rope						
Lead Pipe						
Wrench						
ROOMS						
Hall						
Lounge						
Dining Room						
Kitchen						
Ball Room						
Conservatory						
Billard Room						
Library						
Study						

CLUE SCORE SHEET

SUSPECTS						
Col. Mustard						
Prof. Plum						
Mr. Green						
Mrs. Peacock						
Miss Scarlett						
Mrs. White						
WEAPONS						
Knife						
Candlestick						
Revolver						
Rope						
Lead Pipe						
Wrench						
ROOMS						
Hall						
Lounge						
Dining Room						
Kitchen						
Ball Room						
Conservatory						
Billard Room						
Library						
Study						

CLUE SCORE SHEET

SUSPECTS					
Col. Mustard					
Prof. Plum					
Mr. Green					
Mrs. Peacock					
Miss Scarlett					
Mrs. White					
WEAPONS					
Knife					
Candlestick					
Revolver					
Rope					
Lead Pipe					
Wrench					
ROOMS					
Hall					
Lounge					
Dining Room					
Kitchen					
Ball Room					
Conservatory					
Billard Room					
Library					
Study					

CLUE SCORE SHEET

SUSPECTS						
Col. Mustard						
Prof. Plum						
Mr. Green						
Mrs. Peacock						
Miss Scarlett						
Mrs. White						
WEAPONS						
Knife						
Candlestick						
Revolver						
Rope						
Lead Pipe						
Wrench						
ROOMS						
Hall						
Lounge						
Dining Room						
Kitchen						
Ball Room						
Conservatory						
Billard Room						
Library						
Study						

CLUE SCORE SHEET

SUSPECTS					
Col. Mustard					
Prof. Plum					
Mr. Green					
Mrs. Peacock					
Miss Scarlett					
Mrs. White					
WEAPONS					
Knife					
Candlestick					
Revolver					
Rope					
Lead Pipe					
Wrench					
ROOMS					
Hall					
Lounge					
Dining Room					
Kitchen					
Ball Room					
Conservatory					
Billard Room					
Library					
Study					

Made in the USA
Columbia, SC
24 August 2024

41083499R00067